LAU A R. MURRAY

LOCH NESS MONSTER

ARE THEY REAL?

CREATIVE EDUCATION · CREATIVE PAPERBACKS

Published by Creative Education and Creative Paperbacks

P.O. Box 227, Mankato, Minnesota 56002

Creative Education and Creative Paperbacks are imprints of The Creative Company

www.thecreativecompany.us

Design and production by **Christine Vanderbeek**

Art direction by **Rita Marshall**

Printed in the United States of America

Photographs by Alamy (AF archive, Science Photo Library), Corbis (Bettmann, Dung Vo Trung/Sygma), Dreamstime (Dimaaslanian), iStockphoto (elementals, Matt84, MR1805, Vaara), Shutterstock (cieniu1, Dragan85, Fer Gregory, Victor Habbick, Botond Horvath, Ralf Juergen Kraft, Mike H, Miro Novak, tele52, Serg Zastavkin), SuperStock (Science Photo Library/Science Photo Library)

Library of Congress Cataloging-in-Publication Data

Murray, Laura K.   Loch Ness Monster / Laura K. Murray.   p. cm. – (Are they real?)   Includes index.   Summary: A high-interest inquiry into the possible existence of Scotland's water-dwelling Loch Ness Monster, emphasizing reported sightings and stories as well as scientific investigations.

ISBN 978-1-60818-764-5 (hardcover)   **ISBN 978-1-62832-372-6** (pbk)   **ISBN 978-1-56660-806-0** (ebook)

1. Loch Ness monster–Juvenile literature. 2. Monsters–Scotland–Juvenile literature.

QL89.2.L6M87 2017

001.944–dc23   2016008263

CCSS: RI.1.1, 2, 4, 5, 6, 7, 10; RI.2.1, 2, 4, 5, 6, 7; RI.3.1, 2, 5, 6, 7; RF.1.1, 2, 3, 4; RF.2.3, 4; RF.3.3, 4

First Edition HC 9 8 7 6 5 4 3 2 1   **First Edition PBK** 9 8 7 6 5 4 3 2 1

CONTENTS

A SHAPE

It is a sunny June day. Edna MacInnes is at the lake. What is that huge, dark shape in the water? Edna runs to take a closer look.

THEN IT IS GONE!

4

WATERY MONSTER

Loch (*LOCK*) Ness is a lake in Scotland. It is long and deep. Some people say it is home to the Loch Ness Monster. They call the monster "Nessie."

6

LOCH NESS

WHAT DOES NESSIE LOOK LIKE?

Nessie may have a big body and a small head.

The body looks like it has humps. It may have a long neck and tail, too. **FLIPPERS** might help it swim.

WHAT DOES NESSIE DO?

SCIENTISTS have not found Nessie yet. But they keep looking. They use boats with **SONAR**.

They dive into the lake.

The monster could be a swimming **REPTILE**. Maybe it is a fish, eel, or other animal. Maybe it is not an animal at all. Rocks and logs could look like a neck and tail.

AN EEL

12

STORIES OF NESSIE

In 1933, George Spicer and his wife were driving around the lake. They saw a strange animal. Was it Nessie?

Later, people took pictures of odd shapes in the lake. Some photos turned out to be fake.

People like to tell stories about lake monsters.
The Water Horse is a book by Dick King-Smith.

16

In the book, children find a special egg
near Loch Ness. Then the egg hatches!

NESSIE ENCOUNTERS

Steve Feltham is an **EXPERT** on the Loch Ness Monster. In 2015, he said Nessie was just a big catfish.

But **TOURISTS** still go to Loch Ness. They look for a monster in the water.

What would you do if you saw the Loch Ness Monster?

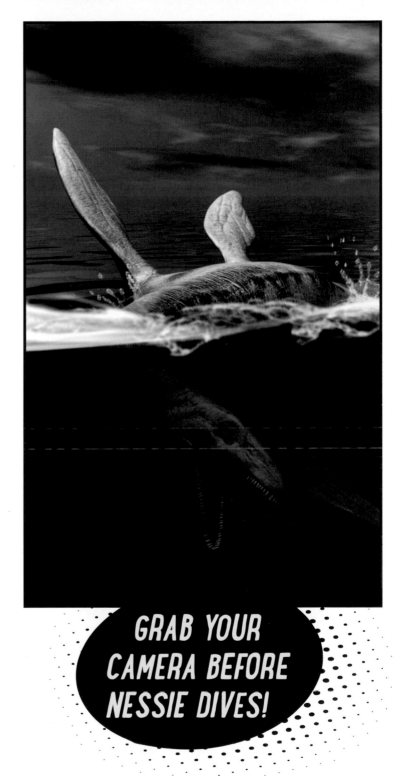

GRAB YOUR CAMERA BEFORE NESSIE DIVES!

INVESTIGATE IT!

A SIGHTING AT LOCH NESS

Imagine that you are on a trip to Scotland. You just saw the Loch Ness Monster! Write a story about it. What did it look like? Were you scared? Will you tell anyone? Draw a picture to go with your story.

GLOSSARY

EXPERT a person who has a special skill or knowledge

FLIPPERS wide, flat limbs

REPTILE an animal that has scales and a body that is always as warm or as cold as the air around it

SCIENTISTS people who study how the world works

SONAR a system that uses sound waves to find things underwater

TOURISTS people who are visiting a place

READ MORE

Lassieur, Allison. *Is the Loch Ness Monster Real?* Mankato, Minn.: Amicus, 2016.

Schach, David. *Sea Monsters*. Minneapolis: Bellwether Media, 2012.

WEBSITES

Loch Ness Monster Sightings through the Years
http://www.telegraph.co.uk/news/picturegalleries/howaboutthat/10776095/In-pictures-Loch-Ness-Monster-sightings-through-the-years.html
See some famous pictures of Nessie.

The Mystery of Loch Ness
http://www.history.com/shows/in-search-of-aliens/season-1/episode-3
Check out a video about the Loch Ness Monster.

Note: Every effort has been made to ensure that the websites listed above are suitable for children, that they have educational value, and that they contain no inappropriate material. However, because of the nature of the Internet, it is impossible to guarantee that these sites will remain active indefinitely or that their contents will not be altered.

INDEX